THE UNSPOKEN OF OUR DAYS

ALSO BY NANCY MANNING

Amethyst Garden (poetry)
Undertow of Silence (fiction)

THE UNSPOKEN OF OUR DAYS

Poems by

Nancy Manning

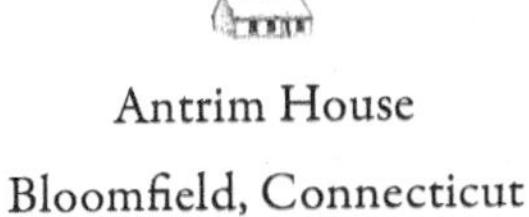

Antrim House
Bloomfield, Connecticut

Library of Congress Control Number: 9798985562101

ISBN: 979-8-9855621-0-1

First Edition, 2022

Printed & bound by Ingram Content Group

Book design by Rennie McQuilkin

Front cover sculpture: "Mother and Daughter"
by Carol Lordi, photographed by Kristen Lengyel

Antrim House
860.519.1804
AntrimHouseBooks@gmail.com
www.AntrimHouseBooks.com
400 Seabury Dr., #5196, Bloomfield, CT 06002

for Kathleen

ACKNOWLEDGEMENTS

Grateful acknowledgment to *Noctua Review* for first publishing "Pulling Away"

My exploring bonds between mother and daughter through poetry manifested itself during my MFA journey. I drafted these poems then and have many individuals to thank for encouragement and feedback during the process of revising them. First, a profound thank you to my husband David and my daughter Kathleen. Your love and support have meant everything to me. Thank you to my siblings for your faith in me. Thank you to the late Harold Robinson. The encouragement from this high school teacher inspired and led me to pursue poetic aspirations. Thank you to the staff at Woodland, especially Jodie, for supplying me a place to create. Thank you to poet Nancy Naomi Carlson for continued encouragement. A special thank-you to the Hamden Poetry Group, my Women's Poetry Group, and my New Haven Poetry Group for your many suggestions on rewrites. A very special thank you to my MFA professors—Jeff Mock, Pat Mottola, Tim Parrish, and Rachel Furey—for the many words of wisdom about writing and the numerous critiques of my work. Thank you also to the many MFA students, who offered their own helpful feedback as well. I am grateful to Rennie McQuilkin, my editor and publisher at Antrim House. A special thank-you to my MFA professor and thesis adviser, Vivian Shipley, who mentored me through this project. Your guidance and friendship through the years have meant everything. I can't thank you enough.

Table of Contents

IV. Winterizing the Flower Beds

V. Deepening Roots

I am silver and exact. I have no preconceptions.
Whatever I see I swallow immediately
Just as it is, unmisted by love or dislike.
I am not cruel, only truthful—
> from "Mirror" by Sylvia Plath

THE UNSPOKEN OF OUR DAYS

I. In Our House of Bricks

Tongue Stuck in My Jaw

title from "Daddy," Sylvia Plath

When I was five, I ran hand in hand with two sisters.
To the woods we went before Daddy's car drove up the street.
Then we followed the leader, skipped alongside Adz Brook.
Nature became our teacher.

We clasped blades between thumbs. Tasted sweet milk
and blew, making a whistle of its tune. Chickadees chirped.
The sun bathed us as we spun god's eyes,
made up stories.

We wandered among daffodils dancing. Pretended to picnic
on a blanket of green, recited rhymes. For supper
we returned home in slow steps, muddied, tired.
That night, fairies streamed

through our dreams, until father's singing like an overplayed
record woke us. He pulled Mother out of bed, insisted
she twirl in his arms. But she was graceless,
a sleepy raggedy Ann.

He wouldn't stop until I kicked, punched.
Back to bed I slid deep, deeper under sheets,
had little air. I hid there, hoped he wouldn't
seek me out.

The next morning, in the hallway, I found
clumps of cotton scattered on the floor,
discarded like scraps. My father, a heartless surgeon,
had sliced open the torso,

left the chamber an empty cavity of Clownie, my beloved
ragdoll. Such a brute. My own pretty heart broken in two.
Through sobs, I vowed never to forget,
never to forgive.

Landscape

I've always hated rainbows. Arrogant arcs,
multicolored from orange to indigo violet,
caused by reflection, refraction, and dispersion
of light in water droplets.

To me, they are exclamations of anger from manic
clouds. My fisted father standing above us—gloating
after a knockdown as he exhaled, claimed dominance
like the mighty Zeus.

Silent as the quiet before a storm, my mother ignored
warning signs, never sheltered below ground, always held
her breath as skies darkened, threatened rain. Cowered
when thunder pierced our ears and lightning bolted

to earth, caused damaged limbs, broken glass.

Home

We lived in the house Father built,
brick by brick on South Center Street.
Like Michelangelo, he plastered and painted.

Carried Mother over the threshold.
Newspapers announced the birth of a son
and then two daughters. His buddies said

he had it all. A family—fed, housed, happy.
Then my birth. We were four too many.
His temper raged. He punched Mother's stomach.

Tore her dress. Her screams made me block
my ears. Back deeper into the ribs of a closet.
There was no heart here, no soul.

For years, Mother covered her bruises.
I affirmed in fiction that her flesh tarnished
black-green-yellow around cheeks, eyes, mouth.

The neighbors deaf, blind. Our priest forgiving.
One night while Father worked, we packed. Clothes,
toothbrush, one doll squeezed into my bag. Mother drove

without headlights to Grandma's. Left alone, Father lost
hope. Rescuers found his body swollen blue, lifeless.
Gassed in the house he had built, by his own hands.

Lilies and Lace

Take the lilies and the lace
From the days of childhood...
This is what I give you
   —Dan Fogelberg and Tim Weisberg

I stroll past my backyard to the old pasture
where you and I played as kids.

Like tin soldiers, we marched
preschooler legs on grassy ground.

On dewy mornings, we skipped
around fairy circles before the sun

forced them to disappear. We took
turns waving taut wrists like the queen

in her carriage on the way to Windsor Castle.
The drawbridge lowered over swampy moat.

On bikes we played bus stop. Delivered children
to South Street School. We strung beads to adorn

our prom gowns made of beach towels pinned
around us. We collected acorns to glue on paper.

Baked pies from air, sifted confectionary sugar
over pastries. Played stick flutes like Pan.

We hopped like water striders though our feet
broke the surface of the brook. We dangled upside

down from Malec's bridge, giggled about boys.
Spied a mother robin feeding her nesting brood.

Tonight I open the birthday gift you gave me
so many years ago—a jewelry box.

Many mornings I danced along like a ballerina
to its simple song. Now rusted on the hinge,

this chest is empty of jewels. And you have
moved on, so many miles away.

Doctor Kennedy

With ready hands you delivered me.
A small town doctor who made house calls
at Noni's home and mine.

Through the years, you charted height, weight.
Squinted eyes through Harry Truman glasses
as your stethoscope scanned for imperfection.
After the squeeze of Velcro to check my pressure,
you winked I was fine. Told me to read Penn Warren.

One summer you began hunching over, stopped
driving the white Cadillac that took wide turns.
A straw hat angled lower over your bald head,
your smile didn't spread so wide.

In newspaper clippings Mom sent me at college,
you seemed thinner, more tired—
such praise for one who saved so many lives.

That morning when at home alone,
you wrapped a cord around your neck
to dangle lifeless from the rafters.
Was it a nod of defeat or a conquering of darkness
you could no longer endure?

down with art

i'm almost six   i don't want to be

here   the bride got married hours ago

why are we waiting? We already ate at this

painting place i need to run   climb   play

follow the leader   tap that statue lady's chest

boobies large as balloons,   naked with nipples

all pointy   on a dare i can hug her

i just need to climb a little and stretch

more   more   she tumbles down   smashes

into pieces   i run fast past that those girls

the guard yells at us but my parents shouldn't

pay   that glass lady was   ugly, ugly

At the Wadsworth

You died on my birthday.
Much of me was buried with you.

Weeks before your funeral,
we spent the day at the Athenaeum, like mother
and daughter. Me in my tee shirt, ripped jeans,
you proper in a woolen suit. Your hair
tidy in an upsweep. At ninety, you never slowed.
My mom didn't like leaving her driveway.

We walked past the Warhol and you delighted in stating
Jackie Kennedy was a goddess of grace. Maybe my mother
would have nodded. I'll never know.

We paused at Caravaggio's *St. Francis*.
You commented that this artist showed
the soul of the man. I leaned closer,
wrapped my arm around you. My mother
would have stepped away before my hand
could have reached her.

You were speechless before Dali's *Apparition*.
Beach emptied of people, the foreground a tablecloth
with fruit bowl. Pears in abundance. The profile
of a dog forming a hilly landscape. Its collar bridging
past and present. Meaning eluded you, so you asked
my opinion. I suggested it represented following our dreams.
You raised an eyebrow. Maybe, maybe.

Over lunch you made me smile. Said I had an observant
eye, spoke wise words. You always cheered me on
even if my poetry seemed obscure. My own mother
brushed aside whatever I created. Disparaged every award
I placed before her in my feeble attempts to please.

Prohibition Ended Years Ago

Go ahead, try to stop me.
Handcuff me, cart me off.
Interrogate me. Confine me to a cell,
pigeon-holed like a letter in a box.
The truth has been exposed.

For here in open field under August
sky at Bread Loaf, I have found
my voice, decided my life.

I will paint in syllables the stories
I have so long held back. I've given
life to the steeples of evergreen,
made them sway like churchgoers
singing glorious hymns. I've captured
the curve of line blowing through rye
like the arc of a cello, plucked
in rhythm to the cicada's symphony.

I've even revealed how your brown
eyes squeeze the skin between your brows.
How your ears aren't open to sounds
of my canvas. How you kept your hands
pocketed every time you listed what
I could not do.

So try now, if you will.
No one can thwart my efforts.

Returned

Rejection stings, swells the flesh,
spreads through body,
burns in memory.

I have your copies, Mother—
two letters: one written by me,
the other by a colleague.
Each addressed to the other's mom.
A pair of birthday gifts.

I wrote about Gail, a gifted
teacher, listener, friend.
My go-to gal, a treasure.

Gail wrote about me.
My word is golden. I help everyone—
students in and out of my classroom,
colleagues, my tennis team, football players
who need tutoring, motivation.

My classes are lively, loud.
I am the life blood in each.
Students feel my hugs.

In the stands, I am peerless.
No one cheers harder.

I am grace under pressure.
A length of steel running through me
despite bumps in the road.

You should be proud, Mother.
Instead you hand back the letters,
mumble, *Take this.*

I look in your eyes,
see winter. Why?

At your feet I have placed
so many awards, prizes
through the years. I ask again.
Nothing.

Who hurt you so that you in turn
hurt me? Was it Father, who took
from you after he took his own life?

Are you bitter, having raised me alone,
doing without to give me
what I needed? What I wanted
most was your love.

I implore you to speak, give me
a sentence, even a morsel
to acknowledge Gail's message.
You raise your chin, look away.

Forgiveness frees a heart.
But you've drained me of so much blood,
my body has trouble replenishing
its own supply.

Best Day Ever

Fear has locked you inside, Mother, so many recent days.
You could be sunburned, stung by a bee, catch cold.
I plead with you to ignore those worries,
spend this summer day with me and your granddaughter
for a visit to the John Hay estate.

We tour the homestead, enjoy a picnic lunch
on the broad white porch. Talk adult to adult
in the presence of twelve-year-old Kathleen.

Strolling in the garden, I persuade you
to hike with us through the woods.
My daughter and I already rambled
it many times. Despite protests you join us.
A feeble smile sours your face.

We follow the Yellow Arrow Trail that
eases down a slope to lovely Lake Sunapee.
Kathleen skips ahead. Cautious of poison ivy
and snakes, we identify white and gray birches,
cedars and white pines, oaks and beeches
like my Girl Scout days when you led our troop
along the Metacomet Trail in Connecticut.

We pause on the thin slice of beach.
Kathleen skims rocks, I soak my feet in the lake.
You sit back, grin. Remark you have delighted
in this day. Never have I enjoyed so much
sunshine in my heart.

Baby Shoes

Mother had them bronzed,
made into bookends—
my first pair, layered
with ruffles, tied by lace.

She ordered a set for each
of us four, an offer she couldn't
refuse from the *Hartford Times*.

She kept them safe—
boxed in a cabinet above the fridge,
until we were grown up.

Now dusty, they have chipped
edges from the many times
I moved, didn't wrap them well.

Still they anchor my novels,
remind me of my mom
and the time when we were
fragile in our house of bricks.

Cairn: Direction Home

Granite rocks—these little voices—
stored in paper bags for when you needed
them, Mom. Carefully, you placed them

in the backyard as trail markers for our Girl Scout
troop to follow. A practice run for the longer hike
the next morning. You had spent that day stacking
them, following a secret code the bevy of us girls
needed to decipher. We required teamwork to find

them, hiking through pasture, downhill to Adz Brook, alongside
gentle waters where we cupped our hands, sipped its cool offering.
Onward, over the wooden bridge, past the briar patch and tossed
litter we stooped to remove. Back across the brook on two rocks
that nearly kissed. Past blueberry bushes, clothed in white tent
cloth like ghostly figures. Berries still too green for us to pick as

we'd done so many times, filling coffee cans attached by a string around
our necks. We skipped to the oaks, planted to mark property lines. Followed
more markers, looped back uphill where you waited, always patient, like a figure
shadowy in the background. A bird ready for flight to rescue us, if need be. Now
these four rocks set by your porch, signal a final message—a note of love--as you
await my visit. Long retired scout leader, you arranged them as a beacon, stacked
largest to smallest, seemingly glued together before your weak heart left you bed-
ridden, your voice barely a flutter, I follow where they guide me, your door.

All That Is Left of You

Your arms seldom hugged,
but your hands sewed buttons,

darned socks, knitted. What I have of you
now is a rectangle of polished granite

alongside Daddy. Engraved cross,
your name, the span of years.

But you were more than that.
Eyes brown. Hair black, thick, curly.

Mouth lipstick Red when you walked
into town. Weekdays when Daddy

worked and my sisters were off
at school, I had your attention.

We'd lean against the washer spinning
its cycle, and play paper dolls, Mary

Poppins and Patty Duke. Outside, I'd
hand you clothespins, jewels bestowed

on a queen. In mid-morning movies,
we'd watch Robin Hood fence across the stage,

Ivanhoe joust for his beloved. After lunch
I'd wash dishes to Big Band songs

on the radio. Tap my feet, move my hips.
You'd hum along in soft whispers.

Under purse pictures, old tissues, leaky pens,
crumpled candy wrappers, a wallet empty

of bills, we'd hunt for tarnished pennies
to squirrel away for ice cream. Weekends

you read from the Shirley Temple Black
storybook. Its cover worn, spine ragged.

I'd dissolve into the illustrations of "Beauty
and the Beast," pretend I'd live happily ever after.

You wondered why I wasted time writing stories.
In your eighties, your memory began slipping.

You didn't know my daughter's name,
but I was still your baby. Death delivered you days

before your ninety-first birthday, awarding you
time, mounds of shiny pennies, lipstick every color.

My Prayer

This I say every night—
Mom and Dad, you gave me life.
But I was a sixth mouth to feed.

Father, too many times I blocked
your blows. Felt your fist. Wished there
had been hugs, words of love.

Mother, too many times you stuffed
in drawers the flowers I colored—
yellows, pinks, reds that ran
outside the lines, when I tried
to brighten your day.

I have so many questions.
Why did you wound me?
Was it because your own wounds
would not close over?
How can I heal?

This I pray every night—
Mom and Dad, thank you for the words
that fill my poems and make me cherish
my husband, my daughter, each of my days.

II. Other Rooms

Following My Own Fate

For Daddy, Mickey lunged the football.
Charlie hooked slimy, slithering worms
with dirty fingers. For Mommy, Carol
wore dresses and bows, helped her clean.

But I was Jo March. Charted my own course.
Sailed to the left when told to keep right.
Thought independently, never stopped reading.
No daughter of Zeus and Themis would control

my sails. My parents couldn't moor me.
I journeyed, docked in my own port.
Attended college, became a teacher.
Have reveled in years of fulfillment.

First Days

Year after year, I stand to face
a hungry crowd. Pairs of eyes staring,
eager fingers waiting, pencils tapping.

I extend my arm. Chalk or marker
delivers a smudge. One word, two.
My name. Cotton mouth.

Finally, words project. Lessons begin.
The square root of eight-one? Stomach
nerves tighten. Little brows wrinkle.

My mother flipped brown flashcards—
cardboard worn, edges torn. Five times five
is twenty-five. Six times six is thirty-six. Night
after night till my head sent me spinning to bed.

I direct my audience. Think of its factors.
In seconds I see smiles on faces. Feel a grin
of my own form. The nod of my head pleases.

Your Presence

For Linda

You would have skipped
at recess, picked me sprigs of lilacs
like other nine-year-olds.

At Oak Hill School, I was
your teacher, caregiver, mother
pushing your wheelchair. Cerebral
palsy crippled your legs. Robbed you
of voice, the ability to reason. Spasms
made you thrust arms. Your eager hands
pulled out your stomach tube. Were you
communicating pain? Hunger? Or did
you have a death wish?

Hand over hand we smeared paints—
blues, red, greens—scene after scene
for each season, each holiday. We stirred
brownie batter, but you couldn't lick
the wooden spoon. You were champ
at bucket ball games. *She shoots, she scores.*
We perfected your dunk shot by slamming
the foam ball through the mini-metal rim.
You had to feel something.

Withdrawn from our program,
you returned to Long Island.
Dutifully I packed your bag, slipped
in a picture of us. How perfectly red
were your cheeks, your eyes peered
out from your little riding hood.

Singing every song I knew, I drove
the school van on I-95, over the White
Stone Bridge, though I was afraid. Many
times I had to pull over, lean you forward,
pat your back like a baby needing to make
you cough up thick phlegm, thicker than milk,
as I had done so many days, so many sleepless nights.

At the nursing home, I said good-bye, kissed
your forehead. Elevator doors closed and your
arms sprang out to me from your tense body.

I knew the words even before the phone call.
Asphyxiated. I pictured your hands outstretched, no
one there to lean you forward, pat your back.

At Griffin Hospital

A twisting of my digestive track,
wrung like rope, bends me double.

I land in the emergency room.

My MRI reveals black bubbles seeping
from an inflamed colon that needs
immediate attention.

Diverticulitis with a perforation.

Years of training have skilled my doctor
for diagnosis, prognosis.

But nothing has prepared him for me.

I can't miss my daughter's going off to school,
my first day, helping at football practice.
Forget surgery, the six-to-eight-week recovery.

I tell my doctor he will witness a miracle.

In the hospital I am treated with antibiotics.
I crawl my way back. Take baby steps
in the hallway. Get my roommate to join me.

On the third day, I rise again.

Swallow broth, stand upright, breathe without
pain. When I am discharged, they line the hallways—
doctors, nurses, the custodian, the cleaning
woman I spoke a couple words to in Polish.

They cheer I will never be forgotten.

I walk, as if on water. Head for home.
Ready lessons. Watch my team claim victory
after my pregame speech about believing.

Hawks

Two red-tailed hawks have left their nest.
I watched them all spring. Body feathers
brown as earth, white underbelly, curved
beak, observant eyes. Fledging flights
smooth, as their bodies grew.

One hawk would study the other, learn.
Eyes flicker from rock to leaf to blade of grass.
Wings expand, talons grab a field mouse.
He flies back to nest, his brother already
there feasting,

and you, my Woodland High student,
fight the fall, try to emerge from shadow
though your spirit hasn't healed. The loss
of your identical twin in a car accident
you witnessed.

Your feet take steps. Earth doesn't crumble.
Your eyes focus forward. Ahead you journey.
Your heart keeps steady. You face each day
as your brother soars. His flight pattern
a replica of yours.

Field Trip to the Mt. Kearsage Indian Museum

Past the dusty arrowheads, empty clay pots,
blankets faded like old denim, this building
houses a haunting treasure. A scene painted
on white buffalo hide, stretched like skin,

framed by feathers. Labeled *Unknown*.
Yellow and red ablaze in a ring of fire.
My students and I lean in, challenge
our understanding. Inside that circle,

a peace pipe offered by chief to men in cavalry blue.
Is this the dream of a nineteenth century Plains Indian
or the nightmare of a soldier tortured by memory?
For around that offering six white men fire rifles.

Natives riddled by bullets collapse, unarmed.
The American flag no afterthought. Destiny
manifest, blood justification for slaughter.

An eagle, bald as an old man, perches above.

If only we could break through this barrier of rope.
Erase the suffering, resurrect the dead, but nails
attaching the hide to surface rust more bitterly,
press more deeply into flesh.

Recruited from Russia

to Svetlana Abrosimova

My Baba and Grandpa Mike arrived by boat
from the Ukraine. Were processed at Ellis Island.
Approval stamped on paper stained with dirt.

Destined for UConn, Svet, you were already family.
My first daughter, adopted, though all we fans knew
was height, the color of eyes and hair. Reporters
informed us you had practiced eighteen years—
bouncing a worn basketball in a cramped home,
shattering dishes, but your mother didn't mind.
You flew here, leaving behind photos, ribbons,
trophies, borscht and smoked fish. You believed.

Wrapped in Husky blue, you powered through
freshman games—up and down the court
in perfect line, exact form to dribble, drive,
lay-up, and jump. An easy two points.

Through two more years you thrilled us
with your finesse and stubbornness.
You were more difficult to defend.
Your stats impressed even Coach Summit.

Senior year you curved your route
more tightly in the paint. Popped threes.
You grew out your pixie hair to shoulder length—
landing you on *Sports Illustrated*—
the woman in red. Our Gampel beauty.

Then Tennessee.
A ligament tear in your left foot.

Coaches guided you to the sidelines.
You were finished for the season.
Doctors performed surgery, gave you crutches.
We were all crushed. Your parents unable to see
you play Senior Night, their first time in the States.

Later, you dazzled as a Lynx, a Sun and a Storm.
Then retired, you returned to St. Petersburg.
Like a foster mother, broken hearted, I lost you.
Though my scrapbook of you spills out pictures
and articles, you remain our two-time All American.

After the Parkland Massacre, February 2018

Inside Woodland Regional High School,
I feel trapped like a caged animal. Pacing
back and forth in my classroom, before the bell
and the arrival of twenty-four teens.

Why continue doing this?

Once again, a school shooting has punched my gut,
suspended my breathing. I can't begin to feel
the grief of these families. So many children,
given too little time.

And they knew the gunman, his history.

I begin planning escape routes—
out the door, down the hall, down the stairs,
through the side door and into the woods.

If not today, tomorrow or the next day?

The bell sounds and students find seats.
We pledge allegiance, hear announcements.
I stand at my oaken podium handcrafted
by a former student. When I look up,

all twenty-four pairs of eyes stare at me.
Waiting, waiting. Though my hair isn't auburn
or pinned up and I'm not wearing a white
blouse, gray skirt or penny loafers like Miss
Jones of Norman Rockwell's painting, I feel the same
tilt of my head.

Our desks are polished wood, straightened
with students upright, silent. My teacher
chair and desk are tidied with gifts of apple
and a rose. The walls wear gray, the whiteboard
is heavy with student scribble. The American flag
is draped above us.

Twenty-four copies of *To Kill a Mockingbird*
are already open. We have Scout and Jem,
Atticus and Maycomb to discuss. A smile creeps
on my face. My students are not afraid.

III. Delighting in Sunlight

Proof of Your Being

Kathleen, your history was not textbook.
At Yale, doctors harvested my eggs, fertilized
in petri dishes with pipettes. There were no test tubes.

With tweezers they transferred ova back into
my womb like the cog of a watch returned
to its rightful setting. Embryos grew
but at one month, all were lost.

Each tiny life a series of misassembled letters
from which I could encode no message, see
no smile, and to which give no hug.

My heart was a glass, dropped,
shattering into millions of shards.

I pieced myself back together to try again.
Photos lined walls of other births, other successes.
Lower my odds after two more cycles.

A hot day in August, new eggs had been
pinched with seed, a third attempt.

Days later I brought home a black and white image
of darkened dots, frozen in time by the snap of camera.
One was you. Microscopic cells multiplying into life.
Hope was thick in the air we breathed.

Then red stains in misshapen ovals plagued
me. Hauntings of what could have been,
never would be.

Weeks later, I lay down, was prepped with blue
gel that warmed my belly. The computer screen
focused on shadow, a blur, a shape. Evidence of you.

Head, torso, arms, legs. You didn't stop moving.
The encasement of skin white as the moon. A heart tiny
as your fist. Circulating your father and me, our blood
through your veins, arteries. A cord feeding you, pumping

you with breath. Coal circles marked your eyes. You may
have seen darkness. But I saw light. A suck of thumb,
ten fingers and ten toes unfolding like a crocus in spring.

Out of Focus

The hospital file documented
your start. Eggs were retrieved,
fertilized, transferred as embryos.
Miracle of modern science.

Later on ultrasound, the monitor
showed hearts pulsating inside
my womb like a neon sign flashing
I am, I am.

One coil joined me to you, another
to Baby B. With delight I twice traced
a head, torso, hands, feet. Hollow dots
marked eyes. Chalky skin needed

sunshine. Weeks later, fingers unfolded,
showed unison with the suck of thumb.
Days later I felt only one kick—
a gush of red signaled what couldn't be

saved. You were a motionless mass.
All I could do was stare at ghostly stillness
that haunted my gut. My tears couldn't
will you back to life. You would not

budge in contrast to Baby B, who aerobic-
kicked, somersaulted in her own space.
The nurse recorded your disappearance,
but it wasn't magic. She held no wand, wore

no black cape. You are memory now.
I keep those early photos in a strongbox
among bank books, car title, will.
A very different kind of scrapbook.

Birth

The sky blossoms pink petals
   of sunrise. A hospital blanket
Warms me. Time's a gentle hand,
   silencing whispers of what is past.
For in this spring light, I hold my new
   born daughter. Her swaddled body.
Rooting for milk, she cradles against me.
   The joys we will share will set
In motion my silent pen.

The Laughter of Children

I want my daughter to delight
in sunlight. My mother hid

in shadows, didn't trust. She raised
me on Commandments her own
mother imposed on her.

Thou shalt not bear false witness.
Thou shalt keep holy the Sabbath.
And other rules—not speaking up,

not swimming for two hours after
eating, not looking outside during
a lunar eclipse. Not opening doors

for Jehovah Witnesses. Polishing
patent leather shoes for Easter and
wearing clean underwear. Running

past Mr. Tate's house because, because
he was a bad man. We didn't believe
in ourselves. Were silenced into

submission. But I want my daughter
to sing, dance, pen her own poetry.
Reach beyond the stars.

The Grand Victorian

I.

Sunday afternoons we'd drive past.
From the backseat of our rusted station wagon,
I dreamed I lived there. Rescued from

meat and potato dinners when Father
exploded like a scalding fire. A mansion
with its mansard of gray slate, walls

of lemon cake, lacy spires, elongated
windows. On the front porch tucked
under a cozy canopy, I read books,

dissolve into gilded pages. Inside,
Mary Poppins lands with her umbrella
to sing and dance with me. Bert the chimney

sweep deposits tuppence into my hands.
We feast on crumpets and tea. On a brass bed,
I sleep in flannel, far from Father's fist.

II.

I bring my daughter to the Grand Victorian,
now a Bed and Breakfast. Golden the walls,
its slate roof and white spires still intact.

We stay overnight not to escape poverty
or any father's anger but to have fun.
We read chapter books on a velvet

sofa. Watch a cartoon video and giggle.
We nibble homemade sugar cookies
and sip warm milk. At bedtime I tuck

her in under the fluff of a lavender
quilt. Turn off the imaginary gaslight
overhead, wish her dreams come true.

On My Daughter's First Christmas

Striesand serenades us as we
lounge before the fire, our newborn
nuzzled in my arms. On the mantel

hangs a trinity of woolen stockings.
Strands of lights spin spirals
around our tree, an angel graces

the top. When you are older, Kathleen,
you will help string the lights, wrap
garlands around branches like the gold

of a queen's stole. You can place the duck
and plaid cat on branches. Add the brown
schoolhouse and tinkle its bell. You can

spell out our names with wooden blocks.
On Christmas morning, you'll be wide-eyed,
tearing open gifts, as a hurricane of wind.

When I was a child, there was always one
gift with my name on it. A doll, a sweater,
a pair of mittens. Our tree silver, plastic.

Discovery

based on Mary Cassatt's "The Child's Caress," 1890

In this book of paintings my mother
gave me, I delight in showing my daughter
each work. One painting captivates me.
It's not the influence of Japanese prints
that I notice first. Nor the swirls of red
central to the background. Instead,
it's the articulation of hands. Seemingly
unposed, a moment on the lap
of the mother's cream-colored dress.
In pastel blue with one black shoe
and the wisps of curl like spring petals,
the child faces her mother, in a pose I don't
recall being in. One pudgy hand resting
on her mother's hand. The second extended—
five fingers probing to detect what?
That Mother has eyes, nose, mouth, and chin?
They are the familiar. Is it to feel
the comfort of breath? To reciprocate
the love of a heartfelt bond?
To imprint a presence that she is?
And all the while with sturdy arms
the mother protects, manifests hope
and dreams. What my own mother
could not or would not do. But this
I promise you, my darling, I will keep
away danger. Kiss every wound, heal
every hurt. Cheer all your dreams. Together
we will remember the unspoken of our days.

Like Falling Flakes of Snow

Yesterday, one, two
   three dropped from
      the apple tree. Today
         three, four more petals

touch down. Six, eight,
   ten, carefree in a breeze.
      Released from nodding
         bouquets of small clouds.

They grace the faces
   of smiling dandelions.
      Dissolve in the sun before
         infant fingers capture them.

The years too have
   dropped to my feet. My
      legs slow to race after them.
         My hands too tired to stop them.

Nighttime Wonder

*based on the art of "Papa, Please Get
the Moon for Me" by Eric Carle*

I flip the page and find a sky unevenly thick
like the blue-black fingerings of a messy child.

All else is glued on, layered. Stars twinkle
on the darkness. A gray-striped tabby runs

through high grass. A tree nearby begs
to be climbed. Smoke wafts from the chimney

in gray wisps of twisted paper. The father
inside, visible downstairs, reaches

for what, a newspaper or book? Upstairs,
the blue-eyed girl in braids with green

ribbons, pajamas, gazes
out her window and wishes to take

the moon from its slumber. Will she fold
it in fourths to fit into her room?

Bounce it? Leash it? Love it like a lollipop?
Dissolve it in her hands like a snowball?

How black the sky would become
without its night light. How lonely the stars.

How a poet like me not so interested in lunar orbits or
phase cycles would lose the muse guiding her verse.

Welcome to Ireland

to Kathleen, age 18 months

Before we drive over the rim
into the bowl of Cork,
steam puffs will greet
you from factories exhaling
summer breath.

The green of the River Lee
will curve through the quays
like a patient hand extending
a greeting on this, your first visit.

Shandon Tower will grin,
tell you four different times—
one for each clock.

You'll see the quick steps
of shoppers, up and down
Patrick Street.
You'll taste the city
buns and butters of Bewley's
and be hooked in.
I'll sip some tea.

Next door the rumble of Bemish kegs
will turn your eye
as the deliverymen roll their barrels
off trucks into pubs.

You can join the patches of children
jumping bricks for a quick
game of hopscotch.

At University College,
where Daddy graduated
you can run through the courtyard.
Pick the wild fuschia,
pose for family snaps.

Then we'll drive
to Slieve Mish Park.
You can see Granny,
sleep in the rowhouse where
Daddy grew up.

Beyond Skibbereen

Along Ireland's Wild Atlantic Way,
a geography of winding roads
narrows through Durus to Ahakista,
like a black line drawn on paper.
A repository of past and present in
modern bungalows and stone ruins.
With lessons to be learned. Other family
to meet. More memories to be made.

My husband and I pause for a pint
at the Tin Whistle. Whooley cousins,
young as the day, welcome my daughter.

We continue on to Kilcrohane
where Granny Eileen grew up.
We drive past the old family dairy,
the school, church, bungalow.
Walk the windy path to the cemetery.
Kneel down at the Daly grave.
Treat the wooden cross with teak staining.
A tradition new to our daughter.

We walk the Goat's Path,
up the mountain of Seefin
where fairies tinker at midnight.

The road turns at the church,
heads up to the Community Center,
curves around a series of farms,
cuts through the granite hills of West Cork.

At the summit, we have weary feet. Need to catch
our breath. The views are spectacular.

To the north, Bantry Bay, Bera Peninsula,
Cara Mountains. One farm stretches below us,
features the stone remnants of an older age.
A house no longer home.

To the south, Dunmanus Bay and the villages
Of Ballydehob and Toormore.

Behind us, seemingly out of place—
a pieta of Mary and Jesus. His death reminds us
who gave us this land well before we knew time.

In County Sligo

Our daughter joins my husband and me as we hike
beneath Ben Bulben. This towering rock left by glaciers,
accordion-pleated atop green limestone. Cold chills

our fingers and faces. Wind roars in our ears. My husband
and daughter converse in his native Irish. "Conas atá tú?
Tá mé go maith." In the rumbling, I also hear the echo

of Yeats and Maud Gonne, in mystical marriage,
strolling here as waves edge gray on the faraway shore.
I tell my daughter to imagine Gonne, a political prisoner

for Home Rule, confined in a cell, extending a hand
through her window to feed a gull. Upon release, Gonne
gallops away on horse, her hair trailing away black,

her dress billowing. Little patience she knew
in childhood, so much more she showed in her fight
for freedom. My husband has taught us so much history—

farmers battled English landowners, were denied
the planting of crops. A devastating famine followed
a potato blight, though the soil remained lush like velvet.

Our daughter reads Celtic myths of leprechauns,
Druids, kings, queens, a beloved saint who rid the land
of snakes. As people open their homes to us, share

their daily bread, Ireland's poetry and history pour
through my daughter's soul like love. The acts
of Gonne and the words of Yeats still alive.

Memorialized

I stand outside the Dublin General Post Office, granite
and Georgian with its hipped roof, transom windows,
stately portico. The British royal arms long removed.

Here Patrick Pearse headquartered twelve men in 1916.
Fought Britain for independence in the Easter Rising.
The building burned, its stone facade remained. I am

welcomed inside. Framed in glass the Proclamation
Pearse read that day. Bullet holes preserved in stone. I
touch them with shaky fingers. The rebels were dragged off.

At Kilmainham Gaol, the dark limestone walls, thirty-three
and a half feet high, are a menacing presence. Passing
under five devils emblazoned in bronze, I enter. Cold

and damp greet me. Silence threatens my ears. Such
a dismal history. On this tour, putrid odors of sewage sting
my nose. Footsteps pound cobblestone. Through miniscule

peepholes, I sneak a look where Pearse was entombed.
Whitewashed walls, straw bed, bucket of water soup, no window.
In the Stonebreakers' Yard, they stripped his clothing. Tied arms.

Blindfolded. Executed. Bulleted body thrown in a ditch
unmarked by name or cross. No priest administered last rites.
Family attended no funeral. There was no resurrection.

Small Ensemble in New Haven

to Kathleen, 15

On a darkened stage, you sit with your oboe
in a semicircle of clarinet, English horn, and flute.
I don't need stage lights to see intensity on your face.
Crease of brow clearly etched, eyes fixed like stone
on paper. Your reed pressed between lips, you inhale
and play. Dressed in black, your performance is
angelic as your fingers dance to Mozart, Bach, de Nazareth.
All ten digits press up and down, lively and directed.

Because of my carelessness, you might not be playing.

When you were four we'd entered the Congregational Church.
I held open the door with my backside. In leaning forward
to welcome back blond little James, who'd missed a month
of playdates, I let go of the handle. The door slammed shut,
crushing your right index finger.

I gathered you in my arms, sprinted to the bathroom.
You screamed in sharp yelps. Your nail unattached,
blobs of blood and flesh, pink, pulpy, were shredded
like my heart. I had done this.

Calm, calm. I slipped the nail back in place and squeezed
the fleshy bits around the tip. Wrapped a wet paper towel
around it and fled to the emergency room.

X-rays showed nothing was broken. But the nail?
The bits of finger that I had stuck back into place?
All was well? I demanded action.

A plastic surgeon who specialized in hands, a Peruvian
doctor, peeled back the dry paper towel, brittle as the finger.
Disinfected, gave a local, stitched all pieces back together.

I asked him what would have happened had he not treated her?
He cringed, looked away, whispered. "Huge risk of infection,
permanent nerve damage, and loss of use in that little finger."

First Prom

The silver ribbon of my daughter's wrist corsage
has faded, the green leaves have wilted, the elastic
band has stretched. The pinpoints of baby's breath
have closed into tiny fists. The double white roses
have shriveled, crepey as my own skin.

Yet on prom night, she was lovely in the grey eyelet
dress we bought together. One of my many joys.
The glitter fell off in sprinkles like fairy dust. Her black
sandals made her even taller. Her long hair, a beautiful
cascade of brunette locks that Rapunzel would envy.

She and her date arrived to the shimmer of a flashy
disco ball and 70's music. At home I stayed up late,
awaited her return to hear stories of who danced with
whom. Unlike my own prom so many years ago when
unasked, I remained home, had nothing to share.

Pulling Away

Inseparable mother, daughter. A duo since
birth when you were first placed in my arms.
I didn't want to let go, didn't care if amniotic
fluid dripped onto my skin. We were bonding.

Daddy cut the cord, but we were still connected—
as you were washed, weighed, ointment rubbed near
your eyes. Photographed, foot-and-finger-printed.
Returned to me. Latching on was easy,

but my milk production slowed. Days later
back in the hospital, yellow skinned,
you were placed under bilirubin lights.
In the morning you were cleared,

slept in my arms, head against chest, a blanket
over us. I gladly stayed home. Read to you,
fed you, changed diapers, scrubbed spit up milk.
You smiled, always smiled. Holding you was my joy.

When you were three, we walked to the gate at Quassy.
You let go of my hand, ran ahead for the carousel. You
wanted the white pony with red roses. I ran after you,
gave the attendant our tickets. With a grin, I lifted you
onto the seat, rested my arms around you.

Years later, I am still running after you.
The space between us ever wider.

Touring Yale, Spring 2018

My daughter and I follow our guide,
pass through black gates of wrought iron
into a quiet courtyard. A privileged world
where co-eds spend this Saturday tossing a Frisbee,
reading on the grass, debating Transcendentalism.

Walking along Wall Street, our guide describes
the Gothic architecture with its pointed archways,
ribbed vaults, flying buttresses, stone gargoyles.
Our imaginations flourish. We search leaded glass,
for Rochester to peer out from Thornfield Hall.
Wait for Heathcliff to dash out a door, tramp
the moors as his beloved Catherine haunts his soul.
We imagine Frankenstein alone in his laboratory playing
the role of God to create the monster of a man.

Outside the Beinecke, our guide reflects
on the school's history of free speech. Back in the 60's,
protests flared into riots against the Vietnam War.
More recently, union workers condemned unfair wages.
Their fists angry for change. Last year, students ranted
about racial inequality, demanded justice for all.

Today, a billboard shouts its message on dark paper,
white block letters:

    "We believe
    Blasey Ford,
    Ramires,
    Swetnick,
    Hill,
    Aguilar,
    Wolf.
    All survivors."

Fifty Senators didn't. I explain that sometimes
we must fight for what is just, even when democracy
has been chiseled away. She responds, "I'll fit
right in. My feet, voice, pen are ready."

IV. Winterizing the Flower Beds

Isaias Aftermath

The sun smiles down
on the sea of my lawn, sodden and sick.
The fun of an angry Thor,

who spit up oak
branches, leaves, pits of thorny acorns.
Stomped on my flower beds,

kicked blossoms to brick. Bruised
cheeks of peonies, begonias, marigolds.
Morning glory on shredded

vines still hide their eyes.
Roots exposed like brown wires untimely
ripped like phone lines.

You shook cedar shakes.
Tossed roof tiles. Punched my mailbox.
Boom, boom, boom. Booted

three trees, knocked them out
like a prize fighter. Mighty will be the effort
to cut them into logs. Reclaim

what was ours. We estimate
the hours and dollars of relief labor.
This silence deafening.

Matunuck Beach, Rhode Island

Under a sunrise tinged with pink,
what I mistake for summer fun—
a sea gull nudging a toy from the sea—
corrects itself in the vision of my field glasses.

The fish whips its tail against sand,
thrusts its fins to flop its body back
to familiar depths as sun sucks moisture
from scales and gills.

The peck peck peck of pulling action
becomes more forceful; a beak made bloody
from battle pries gobs of flesh from underbelly.

After a final breath from the body made still,
a squawk attracts a larger audience that
joins center stage and feasts as water draws

its own dark curtain, claiming what it owns
of bone back to sea.

Dearest Emily—

Your poetry sends me
on a brief carriage ride
through Amherst. I pass

the school, the open field,
the bump in the ground.
At the brick colonial, I am

dropped off at your door.
Words welcome me upstairs.
Inside your room, my eyes view

your garden. The splendor
of lilies, lavender, hollyhock.
The bees buzz and a bird lets

a beetle pass. Globe Roses break
their satin flake. Crimson no more.
When the guide turns, I touch

your desk, knowing you'd approve.
Picture how you sat here—
in your white dress, tippet and tulle.

Delicate your fingers around
a quill. You share a dash
of your soul in swirls of thin ink.

So many snippets I drink them
up like sherry in a glass, a liquor
that is never brewed.

Winterizing the Flower Beds

I start with tiger lilies that tower
over all. Grab clusters of stalk,
trim them down to the base of stem.
as I do in a poem. The black-eyed
susans are next. Their leggy stalks
shriveled to pencil nothingness. I snip
and snip, keep clusters of green leaf.

The catnip has grown out of control.
Its minty beauty overwhelms like bad
hyperbole. It must be simplified, cut back.
The iris once blushed purple; now its
leaves droop in submission. It needs
thinning. Myrtle, far from shy, strangles

meaning with her green arms, stretching
here, there, everywhere. She should
soften the mood so curious bees don't
buzz off. Lily of the valley are fragments
like commas that make me pause, take

too many breaths. I edit them. Lines
of exclamatory marigold need toning down.
I prune orange, yellow, gold. Like extra

words, I rake away cuttings, dead leaves.
Shovel the heap into a compost bucket.

Vermont Village

based on "Over the River" by Grandma Moses

Winter spreads thickly over field
and hills. A frozen river curves through
this countryside as skaters enjoy

hockey. Burdened trees bow down.
A covered bridge allows safe passage
for sleighs on their way to Grandma's.

Red barns shelter animals as farmers
wave hello. Their homes lovely, nearby.
A distant steeple reminds us of a higher

being. A mill shut down for the day.
Its water wheel silent in snow. Far away
mountains nestle for a nap. Easier times.

Outside my window, white dominates
my front lawn. My husband readies
the snow blower. I must hurry away

to answer texts, reply to emails,
plan remote learning. If only the buzz
of breath, neighs of horses, the slice

into ice by metal blade mattered most
in my complicated life.

Visiting Melvillle's Arrowhead Home

Upstairs in this colonial farmhouse,
the study shelves abound with British lit,
the glory of Greeks, tales of the Far East.

Here in Pittsfield, Melville could lower
his model ship from its dust and play first mate.

With Mount Greylock towering
over foliage to the north, he could trace
the curved outline of a beached leviathan.

Remember his epic days of sailing.
Lift his quill and touch the nib to paper.

In daylight, by candlelight, he became
a seafarer and crafted word after word,
page after page to complete *Moby Dick*.

The lure of the South Seas fierce in his veins.
Aboard the *Pequod*, Ishmael and Queequeg harpooned

their spears like Olympians hurling for gold.
The wind mocked their backs, the ropes ate
their hands, the sun weathered their faces like leather.

They rode the waves of Nantucket sleigh rides pulled
by the engine of the beast until butchered.

Using every inch of carcass, sailors cut
off the head and hacked the flesh. Boiled
blubber in caldrons, made oil. Bones

and teeth were shaped into tools, jewelry.
Spermaceti was collected into vats, melted

into creams and wax.
Today when the guide isn't looking, my fingers feel
the top of Melville's desk. For too long I have been Jonah

in the maw of my own whale. Spit out, I can finally take up
pen and whittle a scrimshaw of my own.

Two Georges at the Gallery

*Based on the 1792 portrait of Washington
by an early American and the 2016 portrait
by a contemporary African American.*

I.

Trumbull imagined you at the Battle
of Trenton. A general in uniform—
blue jacket, yellow knickers. Your signet
of red rings pinned near your groin.
No wig, a three-cornered hat by your side.
Your forehead tanned like a farmer's.
Cheeks ruddy. From a distance, you command
your army. Muskets fire on the faraway hill.
Smoke blurs the view. A broken wheel in the lower
corner. On canvas you stand almighty.
Sword ready to free the colonies from tyranny.

II.

Kaphar reconfigured you. We see
your powdered wig, little of your face,
other than eyes and nose. Still we recognize
the white horse, the erect pose of a conqueror.
Extended sword threatening attack. Fastened on you
shreds of cloth, the embattled list of your inventoried slaves.
One strip for each name, attached to your face by rusty
barbs like the nails piercing the statue downstairs:
an enslaved boy decrying the misery of birth.
You fierce owner of whole families,
the boy sees liberty as a shadow.

The Fall of Icarus

to John F. Kennedy, Jr. (1960-1999)

Exploding as a shooting star, John
illuminated our sky, with his great looks
and lineage. His life fizzled out too soon

in the afterglow. America's prince.
Disbelief still plagues my soul,
like a dull ache that refuses to go

away, some twenty years after
his plane crashed off the coast
of Martha's Vineyard. He had no

sun to melt the wax of his wings.
Fog obstructed moonlight. Disoriented,
he struggled to fly. Too lofty his goals

and *George*, his magazine, sadly defunct.

I hunger for more details of his living,
Gone are the sound bites of his biking to work,
rollerblading in Central Park, kayaking

in the autumnal waters of the Atlantic.
How he headed out in tux to a black tie event.
His wife, a glittery shroud, wrapped around his arm

where I dreamed of being. So much
has been disclosed lately. He wanted to run
for office—mayor, governor, president.

He appealed to the marginalized as his father had.
Shook hands and helped the poor. How he dazzled.
As Auden wrote, others may turn away leisurely.

I have nowhere to get to. No place to sail calmly on.

They Call Him Manhole Man

He slumps outside the train station—
against brick, in cardboard home.
Invisible to many.

I stop, read his chicken-scratch. *Help me*.
No hand stretches to pull him up.
His words shallow moans

to deaf ears. His image no mirror
reflects. Grey eyes, leathery skin. His hair
a stringy mop unwashed.

Alone he builds a planet, dwarfed by blanket,
discarded Bud cans, plastic bottles,
a rusted shopping cart.

His jeans, green jacket need cleaning.
I've seen them every time. He pecks at the sandwich
I offer, like a wide-eyed pigeon.

He lives in shadow of days spent below earth in foxholes
No one asks why he waves an American flag.
A dog tag still dangling around his neck.

V. Deepening Roots

On Marlow Hill

News out of Washington is even more bleak.
Pandemic cases spike. No masks during rallies.
Doctors' words unheard. My daughter and I take
a break, hike the trail toward the summit.

Halfway uphill, ponding from the evening's
rain impedes our steps, invites us to witness
stillness until a water strider races across its skin.
Bubbles begin to surface from this oil,

black like night. Pairs of dark eyes emerge.
Three spring peepers surface from this muddy slick,
ready legs. Jubilant in youth, they leapfrog
from edge to edge like children at recess.

Stepping closer, our shadows disturb their play.
They freeze. Rigor mortis stiffens us away.
We head back to our cabin, return to CNN
and the nonsense of adults in office.

At the Beardsley, Summer 2020

Even during this Phase Two re-opening,
zoo animals remain zoo animals.
My daughter and I wear masks,

follow arrows of one-way traffic.
Feel how cages confine wildlife.
Prairie dogs stare, mirror us through Plexiglas.

Beyond fencing, deer freeze as we remain
motionless. Saki monkeys, pale-faced, peer
out from iron cages as nimble fingers fire

popcorn back at us and little eyes delight.
Peacocks strut radiant feathers as if arriving
at the same indoor gala we attend. An ocelot

disappears into bark, as if we never existed.
A gray fox positions himself to pounce
as we lean forward, wide-eyed.

A gator flashes teeth at us. We smile back.
An Amur tiger paces from end to end as we pass by.
Leopard cubs steal some fun as I tickle my youngster.

Our tour ends at the carousel. Music sets our horses
in motion. Allows us to forget the world outside.
Makes us remember when we weren't so caged.

A Mother's Reckoning

We tiptoe past each other,
fill our plates for Thanksgiving
dinner. Turkey, stuffing, yams
potatoes, peas. Absences noticeable—

Great Gram, aunts, uncles, cousins.
Homemade ravioli. At the table,
we remove our masks, offer up grace.
A frown deepens on my daughter's face.

"When will Covid end?"

From my pool of maternal explanations,
I can't fish out an answer. Millions have died
globally, needlessly. When a truck hit Mark,
my brother's Irish setter, left him crippled,

in need of putting down, I couldn't explain
that either. Never again would we walk him.
See him wag his tail. Death is like that.
An unwanted guest, interrupting lives.

I respond that one day a vaccine will be available.
We'll put away these masks, walk around freely.
Death will be halted, made to pause like a TV movie
by the pressing of a remote button.

This I offer, my only words.
My palms open, empty.

Too Many People Await Winter

for Gertie

From the window of my nursing home,
Kimberly Hall, I see October—
bursts of scarlets, flaming oranges,
star yellows, golds could fill a canvas.

Whinnying horses circle the barn, sense
the advent. Nuthatches still gather at the feeder.
Squirrels fill their cheeks with extra seeds.
I don a sweater around my bent shoulders.

The grave maroon of the sullen Japanese maple—
veins stem under cellular skin.
A smooth hand of velvet to touch transforms
into wrinkled fingers, like my cupped palm.

Other patients want winter, welcome the cold of snow.
I long to hear the chirping of spring, feel summer
shower my face, debate Kennedy's assassination,
live for a young visitor to return tomorrow.

Morning in Kilcrohane

Another day of miserable Covid-19 metrics.
I take out a map of Ireland, locate Sheep's Head,
the tip of a finger pointing out to sea from West Cork—
flat, monochromatic, north of Mizen Head.

I remember our bungalow, behind it the gray green
of mountain that beckons me to climb. From above
the fields of serpentine, emerald, aquamarine—
a colorful tablecloth, the land's own mosaic.

Before me, a meadow of white. Sheep pack together,
grazing inside a wooden fence. I count each lamb, drift
into dream-filled slumber. Stroll down to the sea.
A farmer in loose clothes, rubber boots. His staff

a crooked stick he taps in slow pace. A toothless nod
of *Fine day to ye*. A flow of black surrounds him as cows pass.
Butterfly bushes thread their way along the dirt path,
walls of stone. Each blossom a milky torch leans,

smiles in the misty rain. And still beyond, the sliver
of Dunmanus Bay silver blue as the sky
welcomes me as an extended arm to explore its depths,
feast on its fish, drift on its current. The reminder

of this heaven, resplendent. Someday when lockdowns
are lifted, I will return, walk the land once more.

At Otter Pond, New Hampshire

To celebrate the school year ending,
my daughter and I vacation here.

From the porch of this cabin,
we observe the pond, yellow azaleas,

purple irises, one oak.
Unlike trees from our backyard—

uprooted, thrown like spears
during last month's tornado—

this oak remains mighty. Early
in growth, this pillar branched in two.

Somehow it survived. Arms stretch
skyward. Leaves boast a full wardrobe.

Bark, spattered with moss. Its trunk has
withstood winter's weight. Deepened roots.

ABOUT THE AUTHOR

Nancy Manning holds BA and MS degrees in English as well as an MFA in poetry from Southern Connecticut State University. Her work has appeared in an eclectic mix of publications, most recently *Noctua Review* and *Craft Verses Inspiration*. Her first poetry collection is entitled *Amethyst Garden*, and her novel *Undertow of Silence* won the TAG publishing award. She has given readings throughout New England. An avid reader, she participates in two book clubs and three writing workshops. She teaches high school English classes and lives in Oxford, Connecticut with her husband and daughter.

This book is set in Garamond Premier Pro, which had its genesis in 1988 when type-designer Robert Slimbach visited the Plantin-Moretus Museum in Antwerp, Belgium, to study its collection of Claude Garamond's metal punches and typefaces. During the fifteen hundreds, Garamond – a Parisian punch-cutter – produced a refined array of book types that combined an unprecedented degree of balance and elegance, for centuries standing as the pinnacle of beauty and practicality in type-founding. Slimbach has created a new interpretation based on Garamond's designs and on compatible italics cut by Robert Granjon, Garamond's contemporary.

Copies of this book can be ordered
from all bookstores including Amazon
or directly from the author:
Nancy Manning
16 Oakwod Dr.
Oxford, CT 06478.
Please send $18 per book
plus $4 for shipping
by check payable to
Nancy Manning.

•

For more information on the work of Nancy Manning
visit www.antrimhousebooks.com/authors.html.